WORSOOZ

BY CATHERINE KAY

Published by Playdead Press 2017

© Catherine Kay 2017

Catherine Kay has asserted her rights under the Copyright, Design and Patents Act, 1988, to be identified as the authors of this work.

A CIP catalogue record for this book is available from the British Library.

ISBN 978-1-910067-50-5

Playdead Press
www.playdeadpress.com

In Loving Memory of

Joy Kay

Worsooz was first performed on 19th July 2017 at the Baron's Court Theatre, London with the following cast:

Worsooz	Chloe Darke
Alberta	Victoria Winning
Nick	Nigel Fyfe
Anne	Jayne Edwards
Joyce	Kate O'rourke
Geordie	Mark Forester
Matilda/Barmaid/Funders/ Millicent Theresa Harper	Heather Howard

Written by Catherine Kay
Directed by Kevin Russell
Produced by Stephanie Silver

CAST:

Chloe Darke | WORSOOZ

Chloe trained at Drama Studio London. Credits whilst training include: *Punk Rock*, *The Provok'd Wife*, *Midsummer Nights Dream* and *The Acid Test*.

Victoria Winning | ALBERTA

Victoria studied a Masters at East 15. Victoria's theatre credits include, *Vicky the Vegan* (Tristan Bates Theatre), *Necessity* (Brighton Fringe / Bread and Roses Theatre), *If My Heart Were a Camera* (The Battle of Cable Street), *Tremors* (Kings Head Theatre).

Nigel Fyfe | NICK

Nigel trained at City Lit and with the Impulse Company. Theatre includes *Fragments* (Tristan Bates), *The Trial* (Edinburgh Fringe), *Compulsion* (Edinburgh Fringe), *Three Sisters* (White Bear), *Love's Labour's Lost* (Rosemary Branch), *Professor Bernhardi* (Bart's Pathology Museum), *Hamlet* (The Rose Playhouse), *Dinosaur Dreams* (Etcetera), and *Rarer than Rubies* (Theatre503). Film includes *Once Tasted* and *The Funeral Directors*. Radio includes *Apocalypse Slough* (Wireless Theatre).

Jayne Edwards | ANNE

Jayne is an actor, writer and voice over artist. Jayne graduated from Bretton Hall, and has worked extensively creating and performing new work, both scripted and devised. Jayne is an Associate Artist with the Pensive Federation and has performed at The Oldham Coliseum, Tristan Bates Theatre and The Vaults. Jayne has also performed in the 3 minute Monologue Slam at Theatre Royal Stratford East and was awarded the Special Mention.

Kate O'Rourke | JOYCE

Kate is an Irish stage, radio, film and television actress, and co-founder of Spark Assembly. Kate is classically trained at Shakespeare & Company in the US and with qualifications from LAMDA and Thames Valley University. Kate's stage work includes *4.48 Psychosis*, *Dollhouse*, *Othello*, *C'est la Vie*, *Translations, by Mr Farquhar*, and *Birth of a Nation*.

Mark Forester | GEORDIE

Mark studied at LAMDA and after graduating worked closely with *Taggart* creator Glen Chandler, appearing in plays for the stage that Glen created. Other theatre credits include touring with The British Shakespeare Company in *The Taming of the Shrew* and *Macbeth*. Mark has worked in television and film and was co-producer and actor in the indie film *Scrawl*.

Heather Howard | MATILDA

Heather studied at Mountview Academy of Theatre Arts, where she received a BA (Hons). Whilst at Mountview theatre includes, *The Importance of being Earnest* and *King Lear*. Since graduating Heather has been focusing on short films, voice work and work-shopping new writing as well as performing at the Edinburgh Festival.

CREATIVE:

Catherine Kay | WRITER

Catherine Kay is a producer, writer and actress she was born in Manchester (England) in 1973. Catherine studied for a Postgraduate Diploma in Writing for The Stage at the Arden School of Theatre and then diversified her writing for television and film by studying a Masters in Screenwriting at Screen Academy Scotland (Edinburgh). Catherine produced her first play *Bubbysaurus* 'A play about Love, Friendships, Babies and Raves', in 2004 at Contact Theatre Manchester. In 2005 the Manchester Evening News Theatre Awards nominated Bubbysaurus for Best New Play. Catherine produced her second play *Just One Day* 'A play about Sexual Violence and the F Word', in 2011 at Lowry Studio Theatre, Salford. *Just One Day* was written and researched with the support of Manchester Rape Crisis and STAR (Wakefield). The play received 5 stars and was published by Playdead Press. *Worsooz* is Catherine's third play and was written for a wedding present for a close friend. The play was longlisted for the Papatango Playwrights Award 2016. Catherine is currently writing a musical / lyrical love letter to her beloved hometown of Manchester.

Kevin Russell | DIRECTOR

Kevin Russell directed the successful revival of *Hang* by Debbie Tucker Green for the Edinburgh Festival 2016, winning Best production of a Drama and Best Performance in a Drama for Tiannah Viechweg at the *Derek Awards*. The production also played at the Brighton Festival. Other directing credits include the London premiere of the Bryony Lavery adaptation of Henrik Ibsen, *A Dolls' House*, *Memory of Water*, *My Best Friend* (Barons Court Theatre), *Homefront* (Jermyn Street Theatre), *6am Hospital Chapel* (Bread and Roses Theatre).

Stephanie Silver | PRODUCER

Stephanie Silver is a producer at Actor Awareness and works mainly with discovering and aiding new writers and new writing. She trained as an actor at Italia Conti Academy of Theatre Arts Foundation Course and went on to train at The Actor's Class. Stephanie writes and produces her own work through Glass Half Full Theatre, her theatre productions include *The Monologues of a Tired Nurse* and *C'est La Vie*.

With thanks to:

Actor Awareness: Producer, Stephanie Silver and Actor, Tom Stocks, for their support and creative collaboration on the production of Worsooz at Barons Court Theatre (London).

Kevin Russell – Director

Actors – Chloe Darke, Nigel Fyfe, Kate O'Rourke, Victoria Winning

Philippa Edwards for her support and guidance with research on domestic violence

Characters

Worsooz
Teenage Girl (Geordie)

Alberta
Worsooz Mum (Southerner)

Nick
Worsooz Dad (Geordie)

Anne
Alberta's Partner (Mancunian)

Joyce
Manager at Women's Aid (Geordie)

Geordie
Nick's Friend (Geordie)

Matilda / Millicent Theresa Harper / Barmaid / Funders
(Actor to double up)

Note. All characters will speak authentically in their designated dialect.

Staging and Design Notes

The play takes place in Byker in Newcastle and is set in the late 1980's. There are three main areas of action. The pub, Alberta's flat and additional street scenes or monologues can be performed in front of the Byker Wall. The set consists of a minimalist backdrop of The Byker wall with the predominant colours of red, white and blue. Doors and windows in the wall can be used to enter and exit into scenes.

Note. The play is written to be performed and staged as basically as possible, should one be limited by the restraints of a budget.

ACT ONE

ACT ONE. Scene 1

Market Tavern, Newcastle (1986)

SFX. *'Just Like A Woman'* – BOB DYLAN

Nick is sitting at the bar.

He is well groomed and dressed smartly. He diligently studies his crossword whilst sipping from his navy rum and coke. Worsooz enters and jumps up onto the stool next to Nick and flings her bag onto the bar. She is wearing a straw bowler hat and a school uniform with the logo Lady Ellen's.

SFX. *Music fades.*

NICK	E Look a' you?
WORSOOZ	I look like a tit.

She takes off her hat and slams her hand down on top of it.

WORSOOZ	Worzel Gummidge.
NICK	(*to barmaid*) This is Worsooz. She's dead cleva, she goes to that posh school down the road. (*to Worsooz*) How's ya mam?
WORSOOZ	Alreet.
NICK	How's she affordin' that little lot then?
WORSOOZ	The provy man.
NICK	She used to laugh about, everyone that was hanging out. Now she don't walk so proud, now she don't talk so loud about havin' to be scroungin' off the provy man.

WORSOOZ	That's like poetry that.

NICK	Nah, it's five across Dylan. Same thing though.

The Barmaid hands him another rum.

NICK	(*winking*) Thanks pet. (*to Worsooz*) Tell yah mother I've still got her Leonard Cohen record, if she wants it she'll 'ave to come an' get it.

WORSOOZ	Alreet.

NICK	D' ya wanna a bag of crisp.

He nods to the barmaid and she brings over some crisp and hands them to Worsooz.

WORSOOZ	Ta dad.

NICK	How's the school?

WORSOOZ	(*indifferent*) Okay.

NICK	That'll be ya mother, always 'ad ideas above 'er station. What's she doin' with 'erself?

WORSOOZ	She's a manager at the family care centar.

Beat.

WORSOOZ	Dad. / Are you drunk?

NICK	No, unfortunately, I'm stoically sober.

Beat.

WORSOOZ	Dad?

NICK	What lass.
WORSOOZ	What was it like in prison?
NICK	Noisy.
WORSOOZ	Did you have any friends?
NICK	You have no friends in those places?
WORSOOZ	Why?
NICK	Because there's no honour amongst thieves.
WORSOOZ	What does that mean?
NICK	Stop your questions lass.
WORSOOZ	Did ya get scared in there dad?
NICK	(*raising his voice*) I don't want to talk about that place.
WORSOOZ	Sorry dad.

Beat.

NICK	Worsooz, how would you like to meet some of my new friends? And earn yaself a little bit a pocket money like?
WORSOOZ	Doin' what like?
NICK	Just takin' back some clothes that don't fit us properly.
WORSOOZ	Alreet.
NICK	I'll introduce you to some of me pals.
WORSOOZ	Have they been ta prison?

15

NICK	(*laughing*) No lass. You'll get on just great with them.

END SCENE

ACT ONE. Scene 2

Alberta's House

Anne is unwrapping some new headphones that she's bought from Dixons.

ANNE	You let 'er go an' talk to 'im.
ALBERTA	What was I supposed to do? Say no – sorry you can't have a relationship with your dad. How would that make me look?
ANNE	Honest.
ALBERTA	Kids don't want honesty. They want fathers. She needs to understand that missing piece of herself. How can I deny her self exploration?
ANNE	Self exploration? She'll be explorin' the inside of every pub in Byker when 'e's finished with 'er.
ALBERTA	Look, I know he's not your favourite person, but can you try and have a little respect for him.
ANNE	Are you takin' the piss? After what 'e did to you?
ALBERTA	No Anne, I'm not taking the piss.

Beat.

ANNE   How could you let him back in our lives, after everythin' he did?

ALBERTA   I can't keep being angry with him Anne. /

ANNE   He's a fuckin' parasite and he'll tear this family apart.

ALBERTA   For Christ's sake, just leave it.

Beat.

ANNE   / Sometimes I think you loved him more than you love me

ALBERTA   Leave it, I said.   I can feel my breathing going. /

Pause.

ANNE   What did the doctor say?

ALBERTA   The usual, stress and anxiety.

ANNE   It's that job, dealin' with the dregs.

ALBERTA   They're not dregs, they're just poor.

ANNE   Yeah, poor dregs.

ALBERTA   (*smirking*) Don't be contemptuous of those less fortunate.

ANNE   Don't be patronisin' about those quite capable. They're dregs and they think you owe them. (*taking her hand*)

ALBERTA   (*pulling away*) Be careful.

17

ANNE	Of what?
ALBERTA	Suzanne, she could come downstairs.
ANNE	(*sulkily, pulling away*) I'll just sit over 'ere. Put my new 'eadphones on an' listen to a bit of Tubular Bells.
ALBERTA	Don't sulk, it makes you look like a petulant child, and I'm not your mother.
ANNE	I'm not your mother.
ALBERTA	Then we're equal without the Freudian analysis.

Pause.

ANNE	I've written another poem.
ALBERTA	?
ANNE	At least fake interest.
ALBERTA	What's it about?
ANNE	Freezers. Ice Picks for the Masses.
ALBERTA	Ice picks?
ANNE	(*proudly*) Yeah. It's an ironic take on consumerism and the fact that freezers are sposed to save you time, but infact as women we are unwittingly conditioned to be chained to them. (*brandishing a copy of The Hidden Persuaders*) This is a good book.
ALBERTA	(*breathing deeply*) Right.
ANNE	Are you okay?

ALBERTA	Yes, yes. I'm glad to see you've been using your time constructively.
ANNE	I was thinking of reading it at The 'Ropes'. You know, test it out with the general public. What do you think?
ALBERTA	I think... if that's what you want to do, you go for it.
ANNE	Will you come and watch?

Pause.

| ANNE | I'll check out where all the exits are in the room first. |
| ALBERTA | I'll be there Anne. |

Anne leans back and puts on her headphones.

| ANNE | Thanks Albee. |

END SCENE

ACT ONE. Scene 3

Worsooz

My Dad

SFX. '*The Man with the child in his eyes*' – KATE BUSH

Worsooz is brushing her teeth and getting ready for bed. She closes her books at the side of her bed and places them in her school bag.

Music fades.

WORSOOZ
My earliest memory is the blue van comin' to pick us up. That's the last time I saw me dad. We went to live near Northumberland Park, with the Penny People, that's what I called them. We lived in a beautiful Victorian house on Washington Terrace. On sunny days we went on trips out on paddle steamers an' competitions to see who could pick the most elderberries for homemade wine. Sometimes on Saturdays, Sally James from Tiswas off the tele would come to the house to visit Christine. Christine was the floor manager on the Tube.

Beat.

When I was 7 me teacher called us out of class and told us that me dad had left a card and present at reception for me Birthday.

Beat.

For weeks after I cud imagine him watchin' me from across the school yard, as I rolled my 1'rs and 2'rs along the concrete floor. Shimmerin' oils on water, smashin' against my mates' rainbows. In the class if I got asked a question and I got the answer right, I'd imagine him standin' at the side of us rufflin' me hair in the way dads do when they're proud of ya. I felt different to the other kids, I always felt like someone was watching over us.

Beat.

20

When we moved to Seymour Terrace my mam dated Les, the Fireman, he was a shit. Every night after work he'd go for his 5 mile run and on his way back he'd buy a walnut whip and eat it in front of us. One night after his run he fell asleep on the settee. I was playin' out back and got carried away makin' mud pies. Slowly, the sun was gannin doon and it was gettin' darker. I decided to go in the house, I tried to open the back door but it was locked. I knocked and knocked but no one heard us. I ran down the back lane, to the front of the house and banged and banged on the front door. Where would I go? What would I do all night outside on me own? I sat down on the path an' a felt big, heavy tears roll down me cheeks. That's when it hit us. / That's when I realised. / If Les was me real dad he would have heard us knockin'. / If Les was me real dad he wouldn't have fell asleep. / If Les was me real dad he wouldn't have forgotten about us.

How could you forget about yah own flesh and blood?

Beat.

I was made up when I saw my dad on the steps of the Market Tavern. I knew my mum didn't really want me to go over and talk to him. But it was fate, he's me dad. She couldn't stop me.

21

ACT ONE. Scene 4

SFX. *'Heart like a wheel'* – HUMAN LEAGUE

Anne, Alberta and Joyce march on stage holding placards.

Written on the placards are 'North Tyneside's' Women's Aid, End Domestic Violence Against Women and Children', 'Women's Aid, till Women and Children are Safe'.

Worsooz loiters behind, looking unimpressed.

The women begin to chant in unison.

'END DOMESTIC VIOLENCE AGAINST WOMEN AND CHILDREN.'

Music Fades into cheering crowds.

VO. A male voice is heard off stage. 'Fuck Off Dykes, you're spoilin' everyone's fun'.

WORSOOZ   What's a dyke?

ANNE   A very powerful woman.

VO. A female voice is heard off stage. 'Miserable Bitches'.

WORSOOZ   What are bitches?

ANNE   Even more powerful women.

WORSOOZ   This is so embarrassin'. Ah, no. They've got cameras.

Worsooz scarpers as a staunch looking woman, dressed in a power suit with shoulder pads, approaches with a camera crew towards the women.

ALBERTA   Suzanne. / Suzanne, come back here.

JOYCE   (*intervening*) Let me handle this ladies. /

ALBERTA   Suzanne. /

ANNE   We're women, not fuckin' ladies.

JOYCE   Curb the tone Anne, curb the tone. Women
                     or ladies you need someone to project a
                     veneer of professionality.

*As the camera approaches, Alberta slowly lowers her placard in
front of her face. Joyce steps forward to greet the interviewer.*

JOYCE   Joyce Chadwick, Manager at North
                     Tyneside's' Women's Aid.

*Joyce holds out her hand to shake the interviewer's hand, but her
efforts of sisterly solidarity are randomly ignored.*

INTERVIEWER Millicent   Theresa   Harper,   Tyne   Tees
                     Television. You appear to have organised
                     some form of demonstration against today's
                     Viking Festival. Would you like to explain
                     to the general public. Why that is?

JOYCE   Certainly. As you may be aware Women's
                     Aid believe that women and children have a
                     right to live their lives free from all forms of
                     violence and abuse and that society has a
                     duty. /

ANNE   (*intervening*) / DUTY

JOYCE   / A duty to recognise.

ANNE   RECOGNISE. /

JOYCE   To recognise and defend. /

ANNE   DEFEND. /

JOYCE   Defend this right. /

INTERVIEWER What has that got to do with Vikings?

JOYCE   Ah well you see, the word Viking comes from the traditional Scandinavian old Norse meaning of the word Pirate. As our Swedish and Norwegian cousins, here today in their lovely long boats are aware, Vikings or Pirates spent the vast majority of the 8th and 9th century plundering our coastline, raiding, pillaging and raping our women and children.

INTERVIEWER Yes, but what has that got to do with the Vikings?

ANNE   Look Harriet, Millicent, whatever your name is? We think that this event that Tyne Tees Council have organised is a cynical tourism ploy that ignores the truth of what really happened in history. The atrocities that women and children suffered are being normalised, glamourised, look at them all.. they don't even know what they're cheering at.

JOYCE   / Millicent, to answer your original question, we've applied to Tyneside City Council, amongst other organisations to support our funding bid to sustain the daily running of Washington's first women's refuge. The refuge is situated here within the city and for one year has provided vital shelter and support resources for women and children fleeing domestic violence.

INTERVIEWER Are you a feminist?

ANNE (*disdainful*) Yes, we're one of 'those feminists' and yes we hate all blokes. /

JOYCE (*interrupting*) / As you may be aware Millicent, none of us are immune from the potential of domestic violence. /

ANNE / And yes, there's nothing we love more than to grind our Viking axes on 'women's issues'.

JOYCE (*dragging Anne away*) Anne, come along. / Joyce mouths an apology to the interviewer as she steers Anne away from the microphone.

ANNE (*shouting after her*) Did you want to make any more fuckin' presumptions about us Harriet? Perhaps questions about our sexuality?

Alberta accidently drops her placard and glances at the camera like a rabbit caught in the headlights. She picks up the placard quickly and runs off trying to conceal her face.

SFX. *Cheering and crowd noise.*

The interviewer turns to the crowds cheering the longboats.

She smiles and waves to the Vikings and then exits.

END SCENE

ACT ONE. Scene 5

Byker Wall

SFX. '*Nobodies Diary*' – YAZOO

Nick's lament

Nick enters, holding a can of lager and a mug. He opens the can and pours the lager into the mug.

NICK   It was a blue tranny van, I remember it bein' driven, canny fast like. It pulled up outside of the house an' they all jumped out. A fuckin' army of them. Middle class bitches from Northumberland Park, with dead pan faces. They ransacked the fuckin' house an' chucked her stuff in the back.

Beat.

No one asked us what I wanted, they looked at us like I was a piece of shit. / That was my lassie they took. / Me first born. / Never asked us. / She knew she had all the rights. / We have to hang from telephone masts in the public eye to assert our rights.

Beat.

That day outside the Market Tavern, it was fate. I was smokin' a tab on the steps an' she walked past. She couldn't stop us then. 'Mam is that me dad'? 'Can I go an' talk to 'im? She had to say 'yes'. We went to the Fireman's Café across the road, an' she sat there all frozen an' anxious. She smiled politely, like one of them Victorian women, whenever I threw a word 'er way.

But Worsooz, she was carefree, sparklin' like un-discovered treasure. I must have been staring too long, because she became guarded in that way that teenagers do when you pick over their private lives. I wasn't pryin', I just wanted to catch the traces of meself in her face. Traces I hadn't seen for so long, traces I'd been denied. (*swigging from the mug*) Treasure, that's what she is, my treasure.

END SCENE

ACT ONE. Scene 6

The Pub

Alberta, Joyce and Anne are watching the remains of the interview with themselves on TV.

ANNE V.O   'Did you want to make any more…'

SFX. *Beep*

ANNE V.O   'presumptions about us Harriet? Perhaps questions about our sexuality?'

The TV clip cuts back to Alberta dropping her placard and running off.

Joyce lowers her head in shame.

JOYCE   There goes any funding for the refuge.

ANNE It was a joke.

JOYCE Well, maybe if some of us had taken it a little more seriously.

ANNE I was taking it seriously. /

ALBERTA / Why did you have to say it like that?

ANNE Like what?

JOYCE / How many times Anne? How many times do we need to have this conversation? As soon as you lose control they've won.

ALBERTA (*distressed*) / Suzanne, she's going to hear it like that.

JOYCE /As soon as you screech like some disorientated banshee, any intellectual discourse, or political point of any substance that we may want to make. / It's lost. / Do you know why?

ANNE Why?

JOYCE Because then it all becomes about the word FUCK

Beat.

ANNE I thought she found the word feminist more offensive.

JOYCE / That's any potential funding for the refuge gone. You know how hard I've worked to set that place up.

ANNE Face it Joyce, nobody gave a shit about the rapin' and pillagin' of Vikings. They just wanted a fun day out, with a couple of ice-creams and then to piss off home to their fat 'usbands.

ALBERTA I think what Anne's trying to say Joyce, is perhaps we need to rethink our plans for funding the refuge.

JOYCE (*banging her fist on table*) We're going to get funding. That place is going to continue. I've got a responsibility to those women.

Anne picks her Benetton duffel bag up.

ANNE The whole thing was a joke, we were a laughin' stock and I for one am not going to participate in another pointless demo. From now on I'm sticking to performance poetry.

She exits.

SILENCE

ALBERTA Sorry Joyce.

JOYCE It's not a problem.

ALBERTA I thought it was a great idea.

Beat.

JOYCE She's right. It was shit and nobody gave a shit about the atrocities of the Vikings. In their eyes they're heroes, pioneers and conquerors. Who are we to think we can re-write history?

Beat.

JOYCE   Don't worry, Suzanne will be fine. /

ALBERTA   / Nick's out.

JOYCE   Oh.

ALBERTA   He's spending time with Suzanne.

JOYCE   Is that wise?

ALBERTA   I can't stop it.

JOYCE   Do you want to stop it?

ALBERTA   I'm not mean.   He's got a right to know his child.

JOYCE   He's got no rights if you intervene.

Beat.

ALBERTA   I want to thank you for everything you did for us.

JOYCE   You know that the sun will always shine out of his backside no matter what you say or do?

ALBERTA   My cross to bare.

JOYCE   He's done his worst.

ALBERTA   I know.

The lights crossfade.

Alberta exits, Joyce walks centre stage.

END SCENE

ACT ONE. Scene 7

Joyce alone

JOYCE I set the refuge up in 1982. It was the first women's refuge in Washington, Tyne and Wear. / At the time I had a lot of friends who'd experienced male violence, so I did what any self-respecting militant feminist would do. I put an advert in Spare Rib, saying 'Anyone want to do anything about violence against women'?

In the early days I'd be called out alone to a woman's home and I'd face shotguns, axes or batons from some crazed husband or partner. The police would usually hang back outside and let me sort it out. On one occasion I rescued a pregnant woman who had bite marks all over her stomach. After pacifying her for over an hour, she consented to come with me. As we were walking out of the door her husband shouted, 'You don't want to go with that lesbian cunt, children need two parents'. It took all my powers of persuasion to stop her from turning back and going into the house. I believe in putting the survivors' rights at the centre of everything, but I'm smart enough to know that you have to treat the cause of the problem.

Beat.

However, he very rarely realises he has a problem.

END SCENE

ACT ONE. Scene 8

SFX. '*Sweet Dreams*' – EURYTHMICS

Market Tavern

Geordie and Nick are sat in a quiet corner.

Worsooz enters dressed in her school uniform.

GEORDIE   Eee look at her. She's got the look of her father. Your dad said you go to that posh school.

WORSOOZ   Lady Ellen's.

GEORDIE   (*pissed and chuckling*) Lady Ellen's.

NICK   Neva mind him pet. He's a thick twat, 'e neva went to school. They wunt 'ave him.

Beat.

GEORDIE   (*to Worsooz*) I neva knew Nick had a daughter.

WORSOOZ   I neva knew I had a dad.

GEORDIE   I neva knew I had a dad. Ya hear that Nick? I neva knew I had a dad.

NICK   She's sparky alreet. She'll give them shop lasses a run for their money.

GEORDIE   Can ya run Worsooz?

WORSOOZ	Eh?
GEORDIE	If needs be, can yae run?
WORSOOZ	Course I can. I came first in the long distance on sports day.
GEORDIE	(*to Nick*) She'll do for me.
NICK	The girls a good un. The lasses a good un.
GEORDIE	So do you think you'd be able to take these clothes that don't fit us like, back to the shop and get the money back.

He hands her a Burtons bag with clothes in.

WORSOOZ	Yeah.

Pause.

Geordie pulls out a Mercury Maze from his pocket.

GEORDIE	Have you got one of these Worsooz?
WORSOOZ	What is it like?
GEORDIE	The Yuppies have 'em in London.
WORSOOZ	What's the point of that?
GEORDIE	It's a game. You've got to get the blob of mercury into the middle. It helps with their stress.
WORSOOZ	Stress?
NICK	Yeah. They've got to make lots of executive decisions in London.

GEORDIE	Like ya father.
WORSOOZ	Let me have a go.
GEORDIE	Aye lass, you can have it.
WORSOOZ	Yeah?
GEORDIE	It's yours, I've got a job lot.
WORSOOZ	Thanks. What's Mercury?
GEORDIE	Liquid silver and a messenger to the Gods
WORSOOZ	To the Gods?
GEORDIE	Aye.
WORSOOZ	What does she do?
GEORDIE	(*laughing*) She? Well SHE brings messages.
WORSOOZ	What sort of messages?
GEORDIE	All kinds. He... SHE orders people to speak.
WORSOOZ	Yeah.
GEORDIE	Aye
NICK	How do yae know that.
GEORDIE	My wife's a Gemini, ruled by the planet Mercury. (*playfully*) Not so fuckin' stupid now eh?
NICK	Fancy a walk down the Haymarket?
GEORDIE	I'd never refuse another pint man.

Worsooz gets up to follow them both.

NICK   Worsooz, you get yarself off to school.

Nick and Geordie Exit.

The lights crossfade.

END SCENE

ACT ONE. Scene 9

Lady Ellen's School Field

Worsooz is sat alone on the playing field eating a sandwich. She continues to play with the mercury maze.

She pulls out a newspaper from her bag and thumbs through it. Matilda approaches her slowly. Matilda bends down and takes hold of Worsooz's wrist. She places her index finger and thumb around it.

MATILDA   I could have you. I saw you on the TV.

WORSOOZ   That wasn't me.

MATILDA   Yes it was.

She lets go of her wrist and stands up.

MATILDA   What car does your dad drive?

WORSOOZ   A Mercedes.

MATILDA   What reg is it?

WORSOOZ   Can't remember.

MATILDA   My dad's is a C reg. It's only a year old.

Beat.

MATILDA   (looking at the paper) My mother said Margaret Thatcher's been absolutely wonderful for this country. She's encouraged an entrepreneurial spirit amongst the young. What do you think?

WORSOOZ   I s'pose so. I never really thought about it.

MATILDA   You've never thought about it? Britain's first female Priminister and you've never thought about it? What do you think about? Beef paste sandwiches and Gola trainers?

WORSOOZ   What you bein' like that for?

MATILDA   Your dad doesn't drive a Mercedes.

WORSOOZ   Yes he does.

MATILDA   No he doesn't.

MATILDA   And your mother's a lemon.

WORSOOZ   What did you say?

MATILDA   Your mother's a lemon. You stupid slapper.

Worsooz grabs Matilda's legs and pulls her to the floor, jumps on top of her and jabs the top of her right arm.

MATILDA   AAaargh, get off me.

Worsooz continues to thump Matilda's arm. Matilda breaks free and scrambles to her feet.

MATILDA   Look what you've done, right in my TB scar. You horrible, little Geordie witch. White trash, that's what you are.

Matilda runs away, sobbing uncontrollably. Worsooz stands up and wipes away the remnants of her beef paste sandwich from her mouth.

WORSOOZ   (*shouting after her*) Think you could 'ave me now? An' by the way. My mother said that your mother is your father's armpit.

Lights crossfade.

END SCENE

ACT ONE. Scene 10

Worsooz, the take back

SFX. '*Mandinka*' – SINEAD O'CONNOR

Worsooz undresses, dropping her uniform in a heap on the floor. She takes out some drain pipe jeans from inside the Burtons bag and pulls them on. She then pulls out an Arron knit sweater.

SFX. Music fades.

WORSOOZ   The aim of the game is to get the cash back. When I approached the counter I was ready with my excuses. 'My dad bought it for me birthday, he dunt know my size.'

She stands sideways on, sticking out her breasts.

'I'm a big girl now.' She took the jumper checkin' it for faults, turning the cuffs and the neckline inside out, checkin' for tide marks. She even smelt it, the dirty bitch. All the while my heart was going ten to the dozen as she eyeballed me like a potential criminal. Thoughts of being handcuffed and carted off by the coppers, racin' through my mind.

Beat.

Just take the fuckin' crappy jumper back and give me the money you silly cow before I faint.

Beat.

Slowly, she folded the jumper in that posh way that they fold in The United Colours of Benetton, then she held my gaze and uttered the words I didn't think I'd hear. 'Fourty nine pounds, ninety nine pence cash back is it?' Fuck me, I thought, I've done it. 'Thanks very much, that'll do nicely.' Like a cheeky 'ard faced bastard I practically snatched the cash out of her 'ands, before she had the chance to call one of the burly security guards to chase me out of the shop.

Beat.

As I walked to the door I thought about my dad sittin' in the car, I couldn't wait to see the look on 'is face when I 'anded 'im the money. My first take back and I got a whole £50. If those twats at Lady Ellen's could see me now with their posh cars and their private pony lessons. (*giggling*) At least I earned my money and it wasn't 'anded to me on a plate.

SFX. '*Mandinka*' – SINEAD O'CONNOR

She exits.

END SCENE

ACT ONE. Scene 11

Alberta's House

Alberta is napping on the couch. Anne is sat listening to her music with her headphones on.

ANNE   (*lifting one of the phones*) What the fuck's that sound?

ALBERTA   Eh?

ANNE   That noise? What the fuck is that noise?

ALBERTA   (*groaning*) It might be Suzanne coming home.

Anne walks to the window. She sees Nick standing outside in the street.

ANNE   (*opening door*) Have you no concept of time? It's 11 o'clock at night.

NICK   Fuck off back to your 'usband, dyke.

ANNE   My 'usband was a cunt like you.

NICK   Get my wife. I wanna speak to my wife.

ANNE   You're not fuckin' married, you cunt,

NICK   (*thumping his heart*) We're married in 'ere.

ANNE   (*slamming door*) NOB'EAD.

| ALBERTA | Just ignore him, he'll get bored and go. |
| ANNE | 'E's going nowhere, he's just collapsed in a pool of his own piss. |

Nick begins to sing a drunken rendition of 'You were always on my mind' by Elvis.

ANNE	Fuckin' great, now he's serenadin' you. The same fuckin' song that he keeps leavin' on our answer machine.
ALBERTA	Aww, how's he got the phone number?
ANNE	One guess?
ALBERTA	I asked her not to give it to him.
ANNE	Well she obviously listened, just like she listened when she was asked to keep 'er fists to 'erself at that school.
ALBERTA	(*sitting up*) It's my responsibility Anne. Don't you be worrying your head about it.
ANNE	Oh I'm not worrying about it. She needs to realise that scholarships aside, you've busted your arse payin' for all that shit she needs to go to that school. She's fuckin' ungrateful.
ALBERTA	/ Leave it now.
ANNE	I wonder where she gets that from?
ALBERTA	/ I said leave it.

From outside Nick's singing gets louder.

NICK   YOARE   WARE   ALWEES   ON   MY MIND...

ANNE   FUCK THIS.

Anne exits to the kitchen. As she does so Alberta sits up and tries to regulate her erratic breathing.

Anne re-enters and with a bucket full of water. She opens the door and throws the water over Nick.

NICK   ARRHH, YOARE FUCKIN' 'ORRIBLE BITCH, WHAAA'D YA DO THAT FOR?

ALBERTA   (*wheezing for breath*) AAaanne...

Anne slams the door shut. She turns to Alberta who has gone into a full scale anxiety attack.

ANNE   Oh my God.

She rifles through the magazine rack and retrieves a large brown paper bag, she opens it and holds it over Alberta's nose and mouth.

ANNE   Breathe into the bag. / That's it. / In out. / In out. We'll do it together. / In out. / In out.

ALBERTA   (*gasping*) In out. / In...

ANNE   Listen to me, listen to me. / You're going to be fine. / You're doing just fine. / Albee, Albee, look at me. You're allowed to live. You're allowed to live.

ALBERTA   (*gasping*) Just, just, just. / GET RID OF HIM.

Gradually Alberta's breathing regulates.

The dulcet pissed up singing of Nick can still be heard from outside.

Silence.

Anne gets up slowly and walks to the door and opens it.

ANNE   (*calmly*) We don't have any alcohol and we don't have any sympathy.

NICK   Sheee persecutes me.

ANNE   You persecute yourself.

Beat.

ANNE   Go 'ome to your wife. Give the neighbourhood some peace.

Nick stumbles to his feet. He staggers off and Anne watches him till he's out of sight. On the pavement in the garden is left a 12" single of Suzanne, by LEONARD COHEN.

Crossfade.

END SCENE

ACT ONE. Scene 12

Anne's Wound

Anne pauses.

ANNE   He belonged to the old world. He was repressed and sexually assaulted in care homes by women. He described his mother as a retched, neglectful drunk. He studied economics at Bristol University and pulled himself up by his bootstraps and became an educational advisor for Thatcher. /Everything he had, he worked for. / His motto was 'You must always work hard for everything you want'.

Beat.

He chose my step brother over me. / His son was his priority whilst he was busy building his empire. Or maybe he wanted a son built in the image of the man? Either way, the bastard child never forgets the stigma of illegitimacy. He used to say I was special, that I could be a Lawyer. / He'd say being a lawyer is just like performing. The courts your theatre and the jury's your audience. / He justified his neglect with statistics. He thought daughters without fathers were high achievers because the stats say they 'work harder'.

Yeah, because they're driven by the desperate need for male approval.

Beat.

When he died the vultures couldn't wait till he was cold in his grave to divide his money. Money was his power, his definition of control. / He still controlled them from the beyond the grave with his blood money. / He left me nothing, but the motto of work hard for everything you want, and a photograph of him stood in an overpriced suit with

Thatcher. That went pride of place in the bin.

Regrets an inconsolable emotion. The last conversation we had was over the phone. He rang me during a trip he'd taken around the world.

Beat.

From halfway across the world he'd come to the realisation that all the right things he'd done in his life he'd done for the wrong reasons. / 'I've messed everything up for everyone, your brother, you, your mother.' he said.

Beat.

At the time I never understood what he was saying. Now I pity him.

Pause.

All that hard work and none of it came to fruition.

END SCENE

ACT ONE. Scene 13

SFX. '*Breathing*' – KATE BUSH

The Market Tavern

Geordie and Nick are sitting in their usual corner.

GEORDIE	She's a little cracker. The perfect decoy. The girl's a natural.
NICK	She messed up with the take back in Durham.
GEORDIE	Don't be hard on the girl, she had to run and drop the evidence.
NICK	Did you get the cheque books from Dave?
GEORDIE	WhaHay. That postman's a crafty bastard.
NICK	He's a greedy bastard.
GEORDIE	The man's tekin' a risk.
NICK	And we're not?
GEORDIE	Well some of us.
NICK	What d'ya mean by that?

Worsooz enters.

GEORDIE	Ah, 'ere she is. Newcastle's answer to Mrs Bonnie and Clyde.
NICK	(*looking round*) Pipe down, keep your mouth shut. Worsooz, we've got another little job for you.
WORSOOZ	Where's my money?
NICK	What money?
WORSOOZ	£15 Newcastle, Sunderland, Durham for my takebacks?

Geordie discreetly hands Nick the cheque books.

NICK	You messed up in Durham so you can have a tenner. Geordie, give the girl £10, I've got no change.
GEORDIE	Eh?
NICK	Pay the girl, she's risked 'er neck.
GEORDIE	(*begrudgingly*) 'ere lass, treat yaself.
WORSOOZ	(*pointing to cheque books*) What's that?
GEORDIE	Nothin' for you to worry your head about.
WORSOOZ	Why've you got them?
NICK	(*placing in his pocket*) He told you, nothin' for you to worry about. Now listen. Geordie is going to take you on a another couple of takebacks and then you're gonna go shopping.
WORSOOZ	Where?
GEORDIE	(*handing her a list*) Here lass.
WORSOOZ	(*reading list*) Boil in the bag, beef stew & dumplings...
GEORDIE	/ My wife's partial to 'em.
NICK	Worsooz, you're a bright girl, but you need to be keepin' your wits about you. /
WORSOOZ	/ I do keep me wits about me.
NICK	Don't be gettin' complacent. /
WORSOOZ	/ I know what I'm doin'.

NICK	I know that Sooz. I worry for yae, that's all.
WORSOOZ	I won't let ya down dad.
NICK	(*ruffling her hair*) Aye, Yae cud fall in a bucket of shite an' still come up smellin' of roses.
GEORDIE	Come on Lass.
NICK	Look after my girl Geordie, an' don't worry, she'll get your beef dumplings.

END SCENE

ACT ONE. Scene 14

Alberta's House

Anne is setting the table for the evening meal. Alberta is carrying a casserole pot.

ANNE	It's a fuckin' travesty.
ALBERTA	They're expelling her Anne, there's nothing I can do about it.
ANNE	What are you talkin' about woman. Where's your balls?
ALBERTA	Please Anne, I just want a quiet evening meal.
ANNE	This is fuckin' section 28.
ALBERTA	(*confused*) What?

ANNE   Look, (*pointing to newspaper*) 'Promoting homosexuality', like all gay men are paedophiles riddled with aids. / Fuck knows what they think of us.

ALBERTA   It's done with.

ANNE   You can get a fuckin' solicitor. That child she twatted called you a lemon. It's homofuckinphobia. And that school are condoning it for their yearly funding.

ALBERTA   I don't want to talk about it.

ANNE   You 'promote' pop groups. You 'promote' some greedy, expedient, self-serving twat, climbin' the greasy pole. Homofuckinphobia that's what it is. I wouldn't mind but they're all rapin' young boys. (*Alberta cringes*) Rapin' away whilst their wives keep the doylies ironed and the cushions plumped in their fuckin' mansions. Climby, slimy, slimy, climby. Fuckin' Hypocrites.

Worsooz enters.

                I'm sick of these Tories with their 2.4 lifestyles making me feel abnormal. /

ALBERTA   (*trying to pacify Anne*) Okay, do you want to dish up? (*handing her the spoon*)

ANNE   Right.

Worsooz and Alberta sit at the table, as Anne dishes up.

ALBERTA   (*to Worsooz*) Pass the salt please.

Anne sits down.

ANNE   (*to Worsooz*) What 'ave you got to say for yourself? Twattin' people an' gettin' expelled.

WORSOOZ   Mind your own /

ALBERTA   / Suzanne.

Long Pause.

ANNE   (*reading Guardian newspaper*) I see Manchester's just elected the first 'openly lesbian' Mayor in British history.

Worsooz chews her food in disgust.

ANNE   Very progressive city Manchester. /

WORSOOZ   'Ow do you know? You've neva been anywhere else.

ANNE   It's forward thinking, tolerant. (*to Alberta*) I might move back there.

WORSOOZ   Go on then, we're not stoppin' you.

ALBERTA   (*smirking*) Suzanne.

ANNE   (*slamming paper down*) She speaks to me like a piece of shit.

WORSOOZ   When did she make you my parent?

ANNE   I don't give a shit about you. I'm concerned about your mother and you slopin' about the 'ouse all day, under 'er feet.

ALBERTA   Can we please have a peaceful mealtime?

WORSOOZ	I won't be slopin' around the 'ouse.
ANNE	And where else you gonna be? Knockin' around with those scroates from Scotswood? Or with that layabout father of yours?
WORSOOZ	Shut your mouth about my dad.
ANNE	Oh heaven forbid I say a crossed word about 'im, the languishing lord of pisspot. /
WORSOOZ	/ I said shut your mouth.
ALBERTA	/ Since when, since when, have you been going to Scotswood?
ANNE	Yeah, I saw you, really goin' up in the world there.
WORSOOZ	(*stabbing her fork down*) Well, it's better than goin' down for the gravy.
ALBERTA	(*gasps*)
ANNE	Oh now we're gettin' to it. You'd prefer it if your mother had a boyfriend not a girlfriend.
ALBERTA	Stop this right now.
WORSOOZ	No, I'd prefer it if you'd just fuck off because you're an embarrassin' tit.
ANNE	And you're so cool? Tramplin' over your mother like she doesn't exist.
ALBERTA	I do exist... I do exist, I'm here, I'm here.

Worsooz gets up from the table to leave.

ALBERTA	Where are you going?

WORSOOZ   I'm not listenin' to 'that'.

ANNE   Well, she's got places to go and people to meet.

WORSOOZ   You got what you wanted Anne.

Worsooz sticks up two fingers and sticks her tongue through them.

WORSOOZ   A nice quiet night for two.

ANNE   Cheeky bastard.

Worsooz exits.

Pause.

ALBERTA   (*distressed*) Why do you have to do that?

ANNE   Do what?

ALBERTA   (*clearing dishes*) Let it escalate into a slanging match.

ANNE   She needs discipline.

ALBERTA   Do you think I don't know that?

ANNE   Then why do you sit back and let 'er speak to me like that?

ALBERTA   Why do you think?

ANNE   Why?

ALBERTA   Because sometimes Anne, I can't get a bloody word in.

ANNE   So I'm responsible for her shitty behaviour now?

51

ALBERTA	I didn't say that.
ANNE	You let 'er run wild?
ALBERTA	No, I don't.
ANNE	She flies in like a tornado, dumps 'er shit and fucks off. I know what I'd do if she was my bloody child.
ALBERTA	I don't let her run wild.
ANNE	You make excuses for 'er. /
ALBERTA	/ Excuses.
ANNE	/ Yeah, excuses, it's like you're scared of 'er.
ALBERTA	/ What am I supposed to do when she's got a dad like that?
ANNE	You get 'er told. Or better still you get 'im to do it. I'm sick of 'er, 'er attitude's shit. I'm tellin' you now, you sort 'er out or I'm out of 'ere. It's her or me.

END OF ACT ONE

ACT TWO. Scene 1

SFX. *'To Have and to Have Not'* – BILLY BRAGG

Alberta's Flat

Alberta is folding and packing clothes in a suitcase.

Anne is sitting reading the Guardian newspaper.

Worsooz enters talking on an old school Nokia phone. She's dressed in an ill fitting 1980's blouse, that's intended to make her look older than her years.

WORSOOZ	She's packing me case now. I'll be there in about an hour dad /
ANNE	(*to Alberta*) What the bloody 'ells she got on?
ALBERTA	She's been to a job interview. /
WORSOOZ	/ I can't get there any quicker dad.
ANNE	It's not even ironed.
WORSOOZ	Right, I'm goin' now dad. If ya need me you can get me on the mobile.
ANNE	(*to Alberta*) Mobile?
WORSOOZ	It's a phone Anne. Everyone's got them.
ANNE	Well I've not.
WORSOOZ	Spazz.
ANNE	(*to Alberta*) Spazz. That's what I am now.

Worsooz grabs the case off Alberta and shoves the rest of the clothes inside.

ALBERTA   I'll send anything else you need onto your dads.

ANNE   An' where did you get the money for that?

WORSOOZ   FUCK OFF. I don't have to explain myself to you.

Worsooz zips the case up.

ALBERTA   (*handing her knickers*) Suzanne, Suzanne, you forgot these.

Worsooz grabs the knickers and catches Anne smirking. She scrunches up the knickers and throws them at her.

WORSOOZ   A present for you Annie Fanny.

She Exits.

Alberta's shoulders begin to shake and she bursts into tears into a handkerchief.

ANNE   For Christ's sake.

ALBERTA   Now I'm never going to see her again.

Anne fanes sympathy and puts her arm around Alberta.

ANNE   Let him do his bit and you can have a break.

ALBERTA   You mean you can have a break.

ANNE   Yes, I would like a break. I'd like a break from the constant abuse. The never endin' comin' and goin' at all hours. It's fuckin' exhaustin'.

ALBERTA   I've failed her. She's no school, no job and now no home.

ANNE   You've not failed 'er. If anyone's failed 'er it's him. Him 'the one' who's still got a hold over you after all this time.

ALBERTA   He's not got a hold over me.

ANNE   I warned you this would 'appen. I mean why the fuck you 'ave to consider him and his needs.

ALBERTA   It's not his needs it's hers.

ANNE   She's better off without him. He's a parasite. He's fuckin' there all the time, draining us.

Beat.

ALBERTA   I can't just forget Anne. Erase it, like it never happened.

ANNE   I know that. But it doesn't have to rule everything we do.

ALBERTA   So I stay silent? Choose my words and emotions so they're not inconvenient to anyone else.

Long Pause.

ANNE   I can't stand to see you so sad.

Long Pause.

ALBERTA   They're just feelings, they come and go. I can't ignore them.

ANNE   If you want to we could do some more healing later.

Beat.

ALBERTA   (*smiling*) Magic fingers.

ANNE   Your feelings are up here.   Mine are just a
               little bit underneath.

Anne hugs Alberta and exits.

Crossfade

END SCENE

ACT TWO. Scene 2

The Battered Wife

ALBERTA   They'd ask me, 'Why did I stay with him?'

               I'd reply, 'Why did he hit me?'

               They'd ask me, 'Why didn't you hit him
               back?'

               I'd reply, because 'He'd hit me back harder.'

               They'd ask me, 'What does it feel like to be
               hit?'

               I'd reply, 'like you're pulling on a rope.' The
               rope pulls you forward, sucks you down a
               tunnel that's dark, grey and misty.

Beat.

               It's the strangest feeling, you see the ugliness
               in the mirror – you don't want to go there,
               but you know you're lost. There's no light,

no signposts, just him there at the end of the rope.

Beat.

Then he brings you flowers, the remorse, the guilt. He tells you that the florist had asked him if he'd done anything wrong? 'No' he said, 'I just need to show my girlfriend how much I love her. She's so beautiful I couldn't stand the thought of losing her.'

Beat.

But 'I'm lost already,' I say.

'But I found you', he replies. 'Right here on the end of this rope that will keep us entwined together forever.'

'Thank goodness I say, I couldn't stand the thought of losing you.'

What if I was to let go of the rope? Just once when no one was looking. I could forget all the things that he said. All the things he did. They'd lose their energy, they'd slip further and further away. I'd have to feel new thoughts, kinder thoughts, brighter thoughts. Then I'd hear our song playing on a radio in a shop and I'd grasp tightly for the rope again. I'd remember we had a child, all the great things we did all the happy times that kept us together. I'd convince myself everything is pure, everything feels right.

Pause.

But inside I know everything's wrong it will never be right and the darkness I feel overshadows it all.

Crossfade.

Alberta exits and Worsooz and Geordie enter at speed pushing a shopping trolley full of frozen meals and other provisions.

END SCENE

ACT TWO. Scene 3

The Street

WORSOOZ   Down 'ere.

Worsooz takes Geordie through a narrow alley. They crouch down and hide behind the trolley.

GEORDIE   The guard definitely saw us.

WORSOOZ   Don't worry about him, he can't stand phonin' the coppers.

GEORDIE   'As he let you pass before?

WORSOOZ   No, Tesco don't pay him enough to give a shit about us.

GEORDIE   (*picking up dumplings from trolley*) Lush, fuckin' lush. (*looking around*) How do you know this alley?

WORSOOZ   I know everywhere in this city.

She searches inside a small hole in the wall.

GEORDIE	What you own it?
WORSOOZ	(*pulling out a bag from the hole*) Yeh These streets belong to me. Its my city.
GEORDIE	What's that?
WORSOOZ	(*smiling*) Cheque books.
GEORDIE	Where did you get them?
WORSOOZ	Dave, the postman.
GEORDIE	And you're storing them there?
WORSOOZ	Yeah, why?
GEORDIE	Somebody might find them.
WORSOOZ	Nobody ever comes down here.
GEORDIE	How do you know?
WORSOOZ	(*smirking*) They're scared of getting robbed.
GEORDIE	You can only cash one a day in a Post Office, and they mark the back. You know that don't you?
WORSOOZ	Yeah, I'm not stupid. (*showing him the back of book*) See.
GEORDIE	(*flicking though book*) £400 in a week.
WORSOOZ	Yeah.
GEORDIE	How you gettin' there and back?
WORSOOZ	My friend Forestry from Scotswood.
GEORDIE	The Forestry's?

WORSOOZ   Yeah.

GEORDIE   They're gangsters. They give a fuck about no one.

She shrugs.

WORSOOZ   A cheque a day, keeps the debt away.

Worsooz beams a beautiful smile.   Her naivety and innocence shine through.

Pause.

WORSOOZ   I'm lookin' for a new business partner, fancy earnin' yourself a cut.

GEORDIE   Aye nay lass. Your fathers not gonna be happy about this.

Worsooz pulls out a pile of £50 notes from the bag.

WORSOOZ   What he doesn't know wont hurt 'im. He thinks I did a runner in Durham. I did. With his money.

GEORDIE   You stole the money.

WORSOOZ   Well no. I consider that I was bein' undercut, so it was only right I took back my fair share.

GEORDIE   Thatcher's Children? You're your fathers' daughter alright.

WORSOOZ   I don't know why you're bothered about 'im? He'd do the same to you.

GEORDIE   I'll forget we've had this conversation.

Beat.

WORSOOZ   What was he like when he was younger?

GEORDIE   Proud. The smartest guy in the pub. With the best lookin' woman on his arm. A quality woman.

WORSOOZ   What 'appened?

GEORDIE   Unemployment. They closed the shipyards, broke the backs of the unions and silenced the working man.

Long Pause.

WORSOOZ   Why did he go to prison?

GEORDIE   You'll have to ask him about that.

WORSOOZ   He doesn't like talkin' about it.

GEORDIE   Then you'll 'ave to ask your mother.

WORSOOZ   She doesn't like talkin' about anythin'.

GEORDIE   Then ask what's her name...? Her girlfriend.

WORSOOZ   She's a bitch.

Pause.

GEORDIE   He loved your mother. When they got married it was the happiest day of his life.

WORSOOZ   I know.

GEORDIE   How do you know?

WORSOOZ	Well they wouldn't have had me, would they? I'm his treasure.
GEORDIE	Treasure?
WORSOOZ	Yeah, his first born. I sparkle like gold.
GEORDIE	(*laughing*) Is that what 'e told you?
WORSOOZ	That's what he told me mam when I was little.

Beat.

GEORDIE	Put that back in the bag. I think our mans gone. And this little lot needs the freezer.
WORSOOZ	Nah, I'm stayin' here.
GEORDIE	Please yourself.

Geordie checks the coast is clear and exits. Worsooz stays sitting in the alley and gets out her mercury maze.

Joyce enters holding a bucket a brush and posters. She brushes the posters with paste and sticks them to the wall.

END SCENE

ACT TWO. Scene 4

Joyce's Wound

SFX. '*For My Lover*' – TRACY CHAPMAN

JOYCE	My mum was very strict. She bought and sold old houses. At the age of 11 I was stripping wallpaper from walls of terraced

houses. We all had our designated jobs. She did well really, she made her money. / (*catching her breath*) She was a very powerful woman. / People were scared of her.

Beat.

I met my husband in the local pub, we bought a house and I fell pregnant with James pretty much straight away.

Beat.

At first he started off shouting, then the shouting turned to throwing things, then the throwing things turned into things being thrown at me. I was with him for 6 years. I still hate him.

Beat.

The beatings were sporadic, there was no pattern to them. He was a drinker so when he drank they were worse. At the start I fought back. Sometimes I fought for hours, then I learnt, the quicker I stopped, the quicker it would be over.

Beat.

One time he beat me so hard I bled for hours and clumps of my hair were pulled out. After he'd finished the beating he calmly turned on the Nintendo and carried on playing from level 5. I ran onto our street. I ran 8 doors down to where his mother lived and banged on her door. 'He's beat me, look he's beat me', I said. She marched up the road to our house and confronted him. Then she came back and said I was lying and that I beat myself up for attention.

Pause.

'Look,' I said. 'How can I give myself bruises on my back?' (*She pulls up her top to reveal the scars that are still there.*) 'You're a liar', She said. 'He's playing his play station. He'd never do that.'

Pause.

She was a general nurse at the Royal Victoria and managed a support group for battered wives.

Beat.

I'll never forget, one night, I'd cooked the tea. I knew it was coming... I dished it up and he looked at me and said, 'Why are you not eating?' I was six and a half stone, so small... / 'I'll make you eat,' he said. 'I'll make you fucking eat.' / He hit me so hard he dislocated my jaw. I kept putting the fork to my mouth, but it couldn't hold the sweetcorn, as much as I tried to chew, it tumbled from my mouth.

Beat.

That house was claustrophobic. The stench of oppression and hatred. Once a month I managed to save £50 out of my wages, just enough for him not to notice. / I'd get up before seven, when he was still in bed and transfer the extra over the telephone into my friends bank. / He kept my card so that sometimes he could check my account.

Beat.

I planned it, before he came home from work. Within five months I'd saved enough for a deposit on a private flat and then got a man with a van to do the rest. I told no one where I'd gone to.

Beat.

I wanted someone to care for me. But there was only me and my kids. We managed. (*she smiles*) We had an ironing board for a table and when I got a second job I bought an item of furniture each month. The first thing I bought was bunk beds for the kids and then a couch. £350 it cost me. / Pure luxury! I thought I'd died and gone to heaven.

Beat.

When I used to see the psychiatrist at the hospital. He told me to never try to make sense of it. / The reason being, because it doesn't make sense. When he said that, something just clicked. / It was like a big weight had been lifted off my shoulders. I'd never take nonsense from any man now. I've got the upper hand...

Pause.

> No. We're equal. The arrangement is equal.

END SCENE

ACT TWO. Scene 5

The Post Office

SFX. *Police Siren*

Worsooz enters in a hurry, looking around cautiously as the police car passes. She pushes a cheque book through the post office counter.

MATILDA   Don't I know you?

WORSOOZ   No.

MATILDA   Yes I   do... It's, it's... (*looking at cheque book*) Rose McKuen.

WORSOOZ   (*panicking*) I changed my name.

MATILDA   It is you. You're not old enough to have a bank account.

WORSOOZ   Look, it's like this. Me customer. You Saturday girl. Now go an' get my money before I ask to see the manager.

Matilda gets £50 from the drawer.

WORSOOZ   I want £100.

MATILDA   We've only got £20's.

WORSOOZ   Not a problem. Count it.

Matilda counts out the money defiantly as Worsooz fixes her scrunchie in the overhead mirror, unaware she's being filmed on CCTV. Matilda pushes the money through the counter and Worsooz snatches it.

WORSOOZ   Would love to stop and chat, but my dad's waiting outside in his Mercedes.

SFX. *Low Siren, passing outside.*

Matilda waits till Worsooz gets to the exit and slams her hand on the emergency button below the counter.

SFX. *Emergency bell.*

WORSOOZ   BITCH. / I'LL KILL YOU.

Worsooz exits, running up the centre of the stage through the audience.

SFX. *'Little Lies'* – FLEETWOOD MAC.

END SCENE

ACT TWO. Scene 6

The Street

Nick enters with Geordie.

NICK   My Sooz wouldn't do that.

GEORDIE   She's gettin' carried away with 'erself. You need to speak with her.

NICK   / Eh

Beat.

GEORDIE   (*awkwardly*) There's things you need to talk about. /

Pause.

NICK   / My own flesh and blood stealing from me

GEORDIE   Don't be hard on the girl. / She needs a father.

NICK   / Where is she?

GEORDIE   I don't know. /

NICK   WHERE IS SHE?

GEORDIE   I don't know man.

Geordie backs away and exits, leaving Nick alone. Nick sees Joyce's posters and rips them off the wall.

Pause.

Nick turns shouting into the audience.

NICK   Worsooz, Worsooz. Where are yae? I'll find ya, wherever ya hidin' I'll find ya.

END SCENE

ACT TWO. Scene 7

The Poetry Night

SFX. '*Digging your scene*' – THE BLOW MONKEYS

Anne and Alberta dance intimately together. There's a jovial, free spirited atmosphere in the pub.

Music Fades.

Joyce takes centre stage and picks up the microphone.

JOYCE   Power is never given; it is always taken. All women should be able to walk in freedom from male violence. These streets belong to us.

SFX. *Crowd Noise*

The women cheer and clap.

JOYCE   There are thousands of women who cannot be here tonight because they are dead. There are thousands of brave women on the frontline, unarmed, suffering sexual, physical and emotional abuse. This is the world we live in. – WE MUST NEVER GIVE UP ON CHANGE.

Beat.

                 I'd like to thank the wonderful women who have stood by us on this journey. And tonight as we stand here and celebrate our mini milestone, 'our quiet revolution' in our quest for equality and justice, it is with great happiness and joy that I inform you all that North Tyneside's Women's Aid have secured their funding for the next two years. /

Whoops of delight.

ANNE   / Go Joyce, go Joyce.

JOYCE   (*blushing*) / Thank-you Anne. / We'd like to thank our supporters who have also joined us here tonight to celebrate our invisible triumph. We are all living proof that there is such a thing as 'society'. And each and everyone of us have an innate moral obligation to our society and alongside this an entitlement to exercise our right to live the way we choose to live.

Beat.

We owe no one and no one owes us. We are creators of our own reality and in being so, creators of 'our own society'. The state is not our master or our servant.

Beat.

(*catching her breath*) Any woman who understands the problems of running a country should understand the problems of running from a home.

Huge cheers from crowd.

We may often run out of money, we may often run out of ways of generating and finding that money, but we will NEVER run out of kindness and compassion to dilute the current party politics of meanness.

More cheers. Anne stands up on her chair and whistles through her hands, she pulls out a piece of paper from her pocket and signals to Joyce.

JOYCE   Thank-you, all of you for your kindness, okay, okay. (*signalling to crowd to lower noise*) We have a special treat for you all now. Our resident performance poet, is going to entertain you with her new masterpiece. So I'd like you all to put your hands together and welcome to the stage Anne.

Cheering is heard as Anne walks centre stage. Anne takes the microphone from Joyce and Joyce leaves centre stage and sits with Alberta and two other women. Albee's composure appears to be deteriorating and she's becoming fixated with the exits in the room. The cheering continues as Anne clears her throat.

Pause.

ANNE   I'd like to dedicate this poem to my life partner, she knows who she is. It's called 'Lady, love your cunt'.

JOYCE   (*to the others*) / Oh dear God, there goes the funding again.

Anne picks a bag up from the side of the stage and pulls out a Viking helmet and places it on her head. She stands with her legs slightly spread open.

JOYCE   Oh, my God. / Someone stop her.

ANNE   (*pointing at Joyce*) This is for you Joyce.

JOYCE   Jesus. /

Pause.

ANNE'S CUNT SPEECH

ANNE	Lady, love your cunt. Lady, know your cunt. Lady, acknowledge your cunt. Lady, feel your cunt. Lady, explore your cunt. Lady, listen to your cunt. Lady, like your cunt. Lady, enjoy your cunt. (*rotating her hips*) Lady, work your cunt.
JOYCE	Jesus, ye Gods.

The funders get up and leave.

JOYCE	(*head in hands*) We're finished.
ANNE	Lady, VALUE your cunt. Lady, yield to your cunt. Lady, immerse your cunt.

She pushes her hips forward and groans.

Alberta's nervous disposition has increased and paranoia has taken over.

ANNE	Lady, release your cunt. (*she grabs her crotch*)

Pause.

The audience watch dumbfounded, meanwhile unnoticed Alberta still fixated on the exits has gone into a full scale panic attack.

ANNE	LADY, ACCEPT YOUR CUNT. LADY, FREE YOUR CUNT.

Anne groans and jerks her hips, simulating the climax of an orgasm. The exit door flings open and Nick staggers in pissed. The crowd continue to watch Anne's simulated orgasm as Nick stands swaying in confusion at the surreal situation he has just entered into. Anne continues to groan.

NICK	(*spotting Alberta*) Where is she? Where's Worsooz?

72

ALBERTA   ?

JOYCE   Alberta?

Alberta seeing Nick, grabs Joyce's arm as she hyperventilates. Anne returns from her pleasure induced stupor and notices Alberta's panic attack.

NICK   (*to Anne*) Oi! Bitch Dyke! Where's my fuckin' daughter?

Anne jumps off the stage and pushes Nick out of the way to get to Alberta. Nick grabs Anne.

ANNE   Get your fuckin' hands off me.

NICK   What have you done with my Sooz?

ALBERTA   (*gasping*) I can't breathe. / I'm going to die.

NICK   She's fuckin' robbed me! Robbed me, my own fuckin' flesh an' blood, a thief.

Anne grabs hold of Alberta's hands.

ANNE   Albee, Albee, listen to me. / Look at me.

ALBERTA   (*gasping*) I... I... / I can't. / I can't... look at him.

ANNE   He's gone. He's not there anymore. Look at me. / Remember what we talked about? You can move him about.

ALBERTA   (*gasping*) Like a shapeshifter? /

ANNE   / Yeah, like a shapeshifter.

NICK	You fuckin' cunts. / You fuckin' need to know. / She needs to know what she did wrong.
ALBERTA	I can't, he's there. He's colonising everything. Everywhere I look he's drawing a psychic circle around me.
ANNE	He's not there. / He's gone. / Move him about.
NICK	(*to Alberta*) You fuckin' ruined me. You fuckin' broke me, you cunt.
ANNE	(*squeezing her hands*) That's it, that's it.

Albee and Anne hold hands, transfixed and meditating as if in a séance.

NICK	She's damaged goods, only a fuckin' dyke would have 'er.
ANNE	He's gone. / That's it. / He can't touch you.
NICK	Two fuckin' years in a cell. You cruel bitch. Robbin' a child of her father.
ALBERTA	(*screaming*) It's my fault. / I sent him away from her. /
ANNE	NO. / NO, he sent himself, he did it to himself.
NICK	I was a good dad. /
ALBERTA	/ SHE HATES ME, SHE HATES ME.
NICK	I fuckin' loved you, I fuckin' loved you.

ALBERTA   She needed him. / She needed him.

ANNE   / He broke your ribs and ruptured your spleen.

NICK   You were the love of my life, you cunt.

ANNE   (*to Nick*) YOU LEFT HER FOR DEAD.

ALBERTA   I JUST WANT HER BACK. I WANT MY DAUGHTER BACK.

Beat.

She breaks down and sobs. Anne holds her tight.

NICK   I FUCKIN' LOVED YOU.

Long Pause.

JOYCE   (*to Nick*) You need to go.

NICK   (*to Alberta*) One day someone will do this to you.

JOYCE   GET OUT!

NICK   You'll see. / You'll feel like I feel.

He exits. Anne wipes Albertas tears.

Lights slow fade.

END SCENE

ACT TWO. Scene 8

The Byker Wall

Nick enters staggering and shouting.

NICK WORSOOZ, WORSOOZ. I KNOW YA HERE. SHOW YAESELF. WHAT YAE SCARED OF.

Pause.

NICK COME ON SHOW YAESELF.

Worsooz walks slowly down the aisle through the audience holding her bag and faces Nick.

WORSOOZ I'm not scared of you.

Nick runs at her and attempts to grab the bag off her.

NICK Give me that money.

Worsooz pushes him to the ground.

WORSOOZ Look at you scratching in the dirt like a dog.

Nick attempts to grab the bag off her again.

NICK Give me it now or I'll /...

WORSOOZ / I'll what? Do what you did to my mother.

NICK I never did anything to ya mother.

WORSOOZ I know what you are. Everyone knows what you are. I remember the blue van coming for us.

NICK	Blue van, blue van. They took you from me. Bitches, 'orrible bitches.
WORSOOZ	I hear her struggling to breathe in her sleep. She's too scared to dream because of you.
NICK	I give you a home, I fed yae... /

Beat.

WORSOOZ	And a job. / Don't forget. YOU GAVE ME A JOB. /
NICK	/ And you stole from me.
WORSOOZ	I didn't steal anything. I EARNED IT.
	Everything I got from you, I EARNED.

SFX. *Low sounding, distant sirens.*

She undoes the bag and empties the money over him.

WORSOOZ	There take it, it's yours. You need it more than me.

Pause.

NICK	(*whimpering*) Why did ya do it Worsooz? Why did yae do it.

Pause.

WORSOOZ	Because you're my dad.

SFX. *Louder sirens.*

Lights fade.

END SCENE

ACT TWO. Scene 9

Byker Wall.

Worsooz Alone. Lights up, slowly.

V.O Due to your apparent disregard for the law and clear evidence of pre-planned criminal activity across different towns, across a period of time, involving multiple parties conspiring together to commit deception, I'm left with no option than to sentence you to a custodial sentence. You are to be detained in custody for a period of 2 years.

WORSOOZ At that moment it felt like I was in a world he understood. / We had that one thing in common that nobody else in the family had. / It made me feel connected, close. / People had always said I looked like him. My Mam had said it, that made me feel close even though he wasn't around. Made me feel special.

Beat.

On that day I felt connected to him, in a way nobody else was. As they took me down the steps, I watched him until he was out of sight. I was an adult, being treated like an adult, but inside I felt like a little girl. I wanted to crawl inside myself and switch off the lights.

Beat.

As they opened the door to the cell I asked them if my Dad would be allowed to come and see me – / They nodded, turned and banged the door shut. I felt like something in me had died – maybe my future?

Beat.

I know now that this was the beginning of the bridge that I was going to have to cross, on my own.

Beat.

Some people don't know what good looks like, and never make it over that bridge. I have my Mam to thank for that – she brought me up to believe in myself, in the goodness in me, that I was capable of anything.

Beat.

They opened the door and took me to another room. My Dad was there, pacing up and down, like he did. He rushed towards me, hugged me. I held on to him – really tight. The tears came. / It was real. I wanted him to make it better – take it away. Of course, he couldn't. That was my dad. / He never made anything better – ever.

Lights fade.

END SCENE

ACT TWO. Scene 10

The Refuge

SFX. 'Sweet Dreams' – RAE MORRIS (Live from the Quay)

Joyce, Anne and Alberta are unravelling a pink ribbon. They pin it to either side of the refuge.

ANNE   Does it look a bit tacky?

They all stand back and assess it ascetically.

JOYCE   No, no it's fine, it's symbolism.

ANNE   Eh?

JOYCE   Representation of a gift.

ANNE   We're a gift?

JOYCE   No, we're not the gift, this is. It's a gift to our community.

ALBERTA   A well needed gift. That reminds me...

She exits stage and re-enters carrying two small orange trees.

JOYCE   Now Anne, before the MP arrives, please Anne, please.../

ANNE   / Joyce, (*making a zip sign over her mouth*) I'll be the soul of discretion. You won't even know I'm here.

Alberta places the trees either side of the refuge entrance.

ANNE   What are they.

ALBERTA	They're orange trees. It's a sign of new beginnings and good fortune.
JOYCE	It's a beautiful gift. Thank-you, Alberta.
ANNE	Have you got make-up on Joyce?
JOYCE	(*embarrassed*) A little bit.
ANNE	(*smirking to Alberta*) Joyce with make up on.
JOYCE	It's a special day.

Anne, Joyce and Alberta stand back and look at the refuge.

ANNE	(*putting her arm around Joyce*) You should be proud of yourself.
JOYCE	Prides a sin. I did what needed doing. Deeds not words. Deeds not words. We must continue the work of our sisters. The meek do not inherit the earth.

The women stand looking at the Refuge.

Lights fade.

END SCENE

ACT TWO. Scene 11

The Prison

Worsooz is sitting waiting for her visitor. Anne enters and walks towards her.

WORSOOZ	(*under her breath*) Fucks sake.

ANNE	Alright.
WORSOOZ	Alright.
ANNE	I bought you a copy of The Guardian.
WORSOOZ	Thanks.
ANNE	(*sitting down*) What's it like in 'ere.
WORSOOZ	Noisy.
ANNE	Your mother sends her apologies. She was having one of her off days. She's hard work your mother. A full time job.
WORSOOZ	Oh yeah.
ANNE	Has your dad been.
WORSOOZ	No.
ANNE	Probably busy eh?

Pause.

ANNE	Do you want to know a secret?
WORSOOZ	Go on.
ANNE	When I was little I thought my dad was a superhero.
WORSOOZ	Yeah.
ANNE	Then I realised he was just a man.
WORSOOZ	What was he like?

ANNE   Clever, ambitious, rich, fucking neglectful. With him it was a race to get to the top. Climby, slimy, slimy, climby.

WORSOOZ   (*smiling*) With my dad it's a race to get to the bottom.

ANNE   Or the pub.

WORSOOZ   Yeah, there's that.

Long Pause

ANNE   They need us more than we need them.

Anne picks up The Guardian and starts to read.

ANNE   Took me years to work that out.

SFX. '*Suzanne*' – LEONARD COHEN

Fade Out.

The End

Worsooz Comments

This is extremely well written, the characters invite emotional investment and several socio-political themes are explored through their stories. It has an original setting at its centre that immediately draws the reader/audience in. It has some finely detailed characterisation, wonderfully playful dialogue and both touching and funny moments. An extremely promising voice.

Papatango Playwrights Award, 2016

An assured piece of writing, the use of music places the play within a very vivid sense of time and place. The use of songs within the transitions gave a sense of the arc and build of the play. The subplot of Alberta, Anne, Joyce and the women's refuge is particularly strong in the piece and the spectre of domestic violence haunts the whole play and culminates in quite a shocking and powerful ending.

Suzanne Bell (New Writing Associate, Royal Exchange Theatre, Manchester)

There is a feeling of authenticity about some of the material. There is lots of period detail, mentions of Spare Rib, The Hidden Persuaders. I know from reading the play that someone has lived through this era, in this world. It was refreshing to read a play that is political - and feminist.

Janys Chambers (New Writing Associate, Octagon Theatre, Bolton)